CBT WORKBOOK
for Adults

Best Skills and Exercises to Help You Conquer Anger, Anxiety, Depression, Panic. Overcome ADHD, PTSD, OCD. Improve Your Life Healing From Substance Abuse and Social Phobias

TARA WILSON

© Copyright 2021 - All rights reserved.

The content contained within this book may not be reproduced, duplicated or transmitted without direct written permission from the author or the publisher. Under no circumstances will any blame or legal responsibility be held against the publisher, or author, for any damages, reparation, or monetary loss due to the information contained within this book, either directly or indirectly.

Legal Notice:
This book is copyright protected. It is only for personal use. You cannot amend, distribute, sell, use, quote or paraphrase any part, or the content within this book, without the consent of the author or publisher.

Disclaimer Notice:
Please note the information contained within this document is for educational and entertainment purposes only. All effort has been executed to present accurate, up to date, reliable, complete information. No warranties of any kind are declared or implied. Readers acknowledge that the author is not engaged in the rendering of legal, financial, medical or professional advice. The content within this book has been derived from various sources. Please consult a licensed professional before attempting any techniques outlined in this book.

By reading this document, the reader agrees that under no circumstances is the author responsible for any losses, direct or indirect, that are incurred as a result of the use of the information contained within this document, including, but not limited to, errors, omissions, or inaccuracies.

https://www.facebook.com/voxpublishinghouse

Let's keep in touch
Go to https://voxpublishinghouse.aweb.page/self-help-workbooks and subscribe for more contents: everything starts from yourself!

TABLE OF CONTENTS

Introduction 1
Chapter 1: What Is CBT 4
   Seeking Help With CBT 5
   History of CBT 5
   CBT Uses 6
   CBT and Stress 7
Chapter 2: Mindful Practices 9
   Why Should You Practice Mindfulness? 10
   CBT and Mindfulness 10
   Mindfulness and Stress 11
   Mindfulness Can Be Developed in Various Ways 12
Chapter 3: Sleep Disorders 18
   Sleep Diary 21

 Progressive Muscle Relaxation 22

 Stimulus Control 24

 Sleep Restriction 25

Chapter 4: Mood Disorders **28**

 Anxiety Coping Skills 29

 Decastastrophizing 33

 Bipolar Disorder Warning Signs 35

 Challenging Anxious Thoughts 38

 Positive Journal 41

Chapter 5: ADHD **42**

 How CBT Helps Adults Who Have ADHD 42

 CBT and Medications 43

 ADHD Focus Plan 44

 Managing ADHD 49

Chapter 6: Anger **55**

 Triggers 56

 When Anger Becomes a Problem 60

 Coping Skills 64

Chapter 7: OCD **69**

 Exposure Hierarchy for OCD 72

Chapter 8: Eating Disorders **75**

 Self-Care Assessment 77

Chapter 9: Substance Abuse **82**

 Substance Use Assessment 84

 Relapse Prevention Plan 89

Chapter 10: Phobias 92
    Examining the Evidence 93
    Exposure Hierarchy 95

Chapter 11: Trauma 97
    COIVD-19 Trauma 98
    What is Trauma Narrative 99
    Using A Trauma Narrative 100
    Common Reactions To Trauma 103

Chapter 12: Self-Harm 107
    Suicide Assessment 109
    Safety Plan 111
    Stress Exploration 113

Conclusion 118

INTRODUCTION

I would like to thank you for choosing *CBT Workbook for Adults*. I hope that you find the information helpful and useful no matter what your goal may be. In this book, you will find various CBT techniques that will help you work through different problems, including depression, anxiety, anger, ADHD, OCD, PTSD, and substance abuse.

This book is relatively simple and straightforward to use. In the first couple of chapters, we will cover what CBT is and some mindfulness practices that you can use. Mindfulness is a big part of CBT and can help you work through pretty much any struggle you may be having. You'll find several mindfulness practices that you can try out.

Then, the rest of the book is separated into chapters that cover various mental health struggles. We'll go over a brief explanation of what they are and how CBT can help, and then you will find CBT worksheets and practices that you can use to help you overcome these struggles.

These techniques and practices can help you to work through pretty much anything you are struggling with right now. That said, they won't happen overnight. It is going to take time and effort on your part to continue using these practices. If you are currently facing some severe mental health issues, please seek professional care right away.

The best way to use this book is to read through the information and then figure out the best place for you to begin working. Many of the practices will overlap, so while you may not have ADHD, you may find one of the exercises in that chapter to be helpful for your anxiety.

Mental health is just as important as physical health, yet many of us are afraid to admit we need help. People still judge those who struggle with depression, anxiety, and other such problems. They like to say we need just to shake it off or buck up. However, that's not possible. Mental health problems are real. Mental health problems can have a significant impact on a person's health, even physically. Ignoring them doesn't solve the problem and will only make it worse. I encourage you to use this book to heal yourself. These techniques and tools can help you immensely if you take the time to use them. It will make you face things that you may not want to face, but it will help you in the long run. A little bit of discomfort now will bring you more peace in the future. I encourage you to take this step to improve your health. It is a big step, and only the strongest people will choose to take it. That means, if you are here right now, you are a strong person. You are a fantastic person. Don't let anybody else tell you otherwise. You can do anything you set your mind to, so please use this book to improve your life for the better.

Thank you once more for choosing this book. I sincerely hope it helps you.

Chapter 1: WHAT IS CBT

Stress, that's probably something you are familiar with. That's something that everybody knows all too well, especially after a year like 2020. Stress is a natural response in the body, and it can be expected that you experience stress from time to time in life.

However, chronic stress can have a significant backlash on your health. When you are placed under stress for days, weeks, or even months, you risk several health problems. These risks can extend to your mind and body, as well as your emotional health. Stress can also create an inflammatory response in the body, connected with many chronic health problems. This is why it is so important to get help for your stress. There's no way to eliminate stress completely, but it is possible to control its response in your body. Through cognitive behavioral therapy, you can do just that.

Seeking Help With CBT

CBT or cognitive behavioral therapy can help people understand ways to find and change disturbing or destructive thought patterns that have negative influences on their emotions and behaviors.

CBT focus on changing a person's automatic thoughts that are always negative that contribute to and worsens anxiety, depression, and other emotional problems. These negative thoughts that pop up spontaneously can have detrimental influences on moods.

These thoughts can be found, challenged, and then replaced with more realistic and objective thoughts by using CBT.

CBT is a lot more than just trying to find thought patterns. It focuses on using many different strategies to help a person overcome their thoughts. These strategies could include mental distractions, relaxation techniques, role-playing, and journaling.

History of CBT

CBT began during the 1960s and originated with Aaron Beck's work. He was a psychiatrist who noticed specific kinds of thinking actually caused emotional problems. Beck gave these the label of "automatic negative thoughts." He created a process that we now call cognitive therapy.

Earlier therapies only focused on punishments, reinforcements, and associations to change a person's behavior; this new cognitive approach looked at how feelings and thought affected behaviors.

Since that time, CBT has become an effective treatment for a large variety of conditions and disorders.

CBT is the most researched kind of therapy because treatments are focused on very specific goals, and the results could be measured very easily.

CBT could be a great treatment choice for many different psychological problems. If you think that you could benefit from this kind of therapy, talk to your doctor and see if they can refer you to a trained therapist.

CBT Uses

CBT can be an effective tool when used as a short-term treatment that centers on helping people who have a certain problem. It teaches them to focus on their present beliefs and thoughts. CBT can be used to treat a large range of issues, including:

- Stress
- Phobias
- Personality disorders
- Panic attacks
- Eating disorders
- Depression
- Bipolar disorder
- Anxiety

- Anger issues
- Addictions

CBT is very focused and goal-oriented, and your therapist will have a very active role. You will work with your therapist toward goals that you both have worked to establish. Your therapist will explain the process in great detail. They will probably give you some homework to do in between your sessions.

CBT and Stress

A hormonal response creates stress. The hypothalamus gets fired up when you experience stress and sends signals throughout your nervous system. Once the kidneys receive that message, they will release stress hormones, namely cortisol and adrenaline. Stress fills your mind with incessant worries and is often unjustified. Your mind is filled with thoughts about what you have to do and what your future may hold. Rather than focusing on what you need to, these thoughts bombard your mind, and it's hard to get away from them.

Through the use of CBT, you can learn:

- Why certain situations are creating stress for you
- Learn about certain thinking patterns you hold that could be keeping you stuck.
- Discover how to think and behave in a new way that can get rid of the stress.

- Come up with a new understanding and confidence in your ability to face those stressful situations.

The amazing thing with CBT is, it can help with several other health issues other than stress, but the tools tend to remain the same. CBT therapy for stress helps you to learn more about things that increase your stress levels. It can also help you learn new ways of thinking and acting to help you spot triggers and improve your confidence to deal with stressful moments more effectively. After working through CBT tools a few times, you will start to feel more at ease, in control, and like you handle life better.

While unpleasant, stress isn't an illness. However, stress has been connected to many mental health conditions, including PTSD, psychosis, anxiety, and depression. That's why, while there may not be a specific chapter concerning stress, the worksheets and tools within those chapters can help you deal with stress and live a happier life.

Chapter 2:
MINDFUL PRACTICES

To quote Jon Kabat-Zinn, "Mindfulness means paying attention in a particular way: on purpose, in the present moment, and nonjudgmentally."

Another definition comes from Scott Bishop, who is a psychologist. He describes being mindful as a present-centered, nonjudgmental, elaborate awareness where every sensation, feeling, and thought that comes up is acknowledged and accepted for what it is.

This might sound simple, but mindfulness can change the way we relate to experiences and events. It can create a better way of living in the world that will make us happier and less reactive.

Why Should You Practice Mindfulness?

For many people practicing mindfulness is an excellent way to enhance their performance or health. Other people use it to explore themselves. And still, others use it as a part of their spirituality to bring them closer to their "divine truth."

It doesn't matter what a person's motivation is; research has shown that practicing mindfulness can change the brain's functions and structure and change how we respond to stress. This suggests that mindfulness can greatly impact our emotional and physical health that would be worth looking at.

CBT and Mindfulness

CBT commonly uses mindfulness. This is known as mindfulness-based cognitive therapy or MBCT. It is a type of psychotherapy that combines meditation, cognitive therapy, and the cultivation of a present-oriented attitude known as mindfulness.

Cognitive therapy's main assumption is that thoughts come before moods and that having false self-beliefs will create negative emotions. Cognitive therapy's main goal is to help you reassess and recognize your negative thought patterns and replace them that are more positive and closer to reality.

Mindfulness-based cognitive therapy will build upon these basic principles by using mindfulness meditation to help people pay more attention to their feelings and thoughts without judging them.

For example, a person who has chronic depression can use mindfulness to avoid relapses by learning how to not engage with their automatic thought patterns that cause their depression to become worse. It has been proven that mindfulness can, on average, reduce the risk of a depression relapse by 50%, no matter the person's education, age, sex, or relationship status.

Mindfulness and Stress

Mindfulness is also a powerful tool for reducing stress, which we've already discussed everybody has. There is growing evidence from numerous studies done by hundreds of universities that show mindfulness helps to gently build inner strength so that future stressors don't have a strong impact on our physical and mental wellbeing.

Why is mindfulness so great for stress? Here are nine reasons why.

1. You notice your thoughts – You will learn how to take a step back from your thoughts and not take them literally. This will prevent your stress response from being initiated.
2. You won't immediately react to a situation – Instead, you will find you have a moment to stop and think and reach a healthy solution.
3. Mindfulness will switch on your "being" mode – This mode is closely connected with relaxation. The opposite of this is your "doing" mode and is connected with your stress response.

4. You become more aware of your needs – You might notice a pain quicker and take the correct course of action.
5. You notice others' emotions – As you increase your emotional intelligence, you are less likely to face conflicts.
6. Your level of compassion and care for yourself and others grow – A compassionate mind helps to inhibit and soothe the stress response.
7. Mindfulness reduces brain activity in the amygdale – The amygdale is a big player in your stress response, so your stress will be reduced.
8. You can focus better – This will help you do your work more efficiently, and it will improve your sense of well-being and lowers your stress response.
9. You can change your attitude to stress – Instead of only seeing the negative consequences of feeling stressed, mindfulness will provide you an area of space to think differently about stress.

Mindfulness Can Be Developed in Various Ways

If mindfulness is so helpful, how can people learn to develop this skill? Various practices help support developing mindfulness, including being in nature, movement, and meditation. This chapter describes some of these meditation techniques, but generally, they try to develop the three main characteristics of mindfulness:

- An attitude that is kind, curious, and doesn't judge

- Attention to the things that are happening around you
- Intention to create awareness

To help you cultivate a mindfulness practice, the following are some various ways to help cultivate mindfulness. It is helpful to use mindfulness along with the other techniques that are discussed in this book. It all works together to help improve your mental wellbeing.

Mindful Breathing to Begin Your Day

Set your alarm clock for either five or ten minutes earlier than when you typically get up. Once the alarm goes off, sit up and get comfortable. You are going to use this time to enjoy some centering breathing. This is one of the best ways to start your day. You will be getting up at the right time, and you aren't sacrificing any time from your normal routine. When you practice mindfulness during morning hours, you are starting your day feeling clear-headed, refreshed, and calm. It allows you to wake up instead of jumping right out of bed and having to rush around right from the start gently.

You can close your eyes if you would like. When I keep my eyes open, I find that I need to take care of that just defeats the whole purpose of this exercise. Breathe in deeply and notice the sensation of your breath filling your lungs. Breathe out, and breathe in again. You might realize your mind wanders off here and there, but that is okay. Just gently bring it back to your breath.

With some time and practice, this will get easier. You can set a timer for five or ten minutes. You don't need to do this longer than that.

Pick A Task To Mindfully Do
You probably have a page full of things you would like to get done. Those tasks give you the best chance to bring more mindfulness into your life.

Look at these ideas:

- Take a walk while mindfully noticing all of the sounds that are happening around you. Notice how the ground feels as you are walking, or look for things that you may have never seen before.
- Take a mindful shower by observing the sensations of the water running down your body.
- Drink your morning coffee or tea mindfully. This means that you will need to put your phone away and then notice its tastes, temperature, flavor, and aroma.

The idea of doing this activity is to start creating a habit of doing something that is simple, that you would already be doing every day, but in a new, mindful way. Release all of the distractions as your work to focus on the present moment.

Allow Yourself To Feel Your Emotions Without Judging Them
This is a great activity to take part in at the end of the day and check in on your needs. You can do this simply by asking yourself, "How

am I feeling right now?" If you can, try to give yourself a couple of minutes each day to observe your emotions while creating a space where you can experience them.

You could find a quiet place and focus all of your attention inside of you.

Take a moment to notice how you physically feel.

Think about the events that happened to you that day.

Notice any emotions you might have and why they are there.

Now, release those reasons and focus solely on the emotion. You might encounter something like: "I feel irritated because the house is a mess and my boss expects too much out of me." You can break this down into: "I feel irritated."

Notice how it feels to be irritated without judging yourself for that feeling. Let yourself really feel that emotion, and it might be fading away.

Have a Mindful Conversation With Someone You Love
Connecting with others is key to feeling heard, supported, and loved. Why not make a point of adding some mindfulness into your relationship to bring the two of you closer?

Here is how you can do this:

- Ask someone you love if they have time to talk. Tell them that you would really like to hear how their week was and let them

- know that you want to have a conversation with them without distractions like phones or television.

- You can also decide to go out to someplace nice like a restaurant where you can have something to eat and talk about, or you could just for a walk.

- You intend to give your attention and time to your loved ones while being open-minded while they are talking.

- When you have finished talking, compliment the person. Tell them that you appreciate their openness, honesty, and time.

Do Something Creative

Coloring, play an instrument, plan a trip, build things, sew, cook, write, garden, or paint… there are so many ways you can express your creativity.

Anytime you can immerse yourself into a creative activity, you are experiencing mindfulness. You don't think about anything but what you are doing at that moment because you are too focused on taking part in the activity.

The other week I decided to plant some new tulip bulbs. I headed out to the garden and placed the bulbs on top of the ground to see if I liked where they were placed. It took me a couple of times to get them exactly how I wanted them. I wasn't thinking about my unread emails, what I would cook for dinner, or thinking about that to-do list hanging on the fridge. I was only paying attention to my flowers I would enjoy in the spring. I was completely immersed in gardening. While we are on the subject of nature:

Spend Some Time In Nature

When you are out in nature, it isn't just a great way to add some mindfulness into your world, but you get to experience numerous other benefits, too.

One study done in 2019 discovered that spending only two hours outside every week could help with a person's wellbeing and health. This study involved more than 20,000 participants, and those who spent two hours in nature didn't experience mental health disorders or poor health such as cardiovascular disease and obesity. The time that they spent in nature didn't even have to be physical. It could be as simple as sitting on a park bench and just enjoying the view.

Another study showed that spending 20 minutes in nature could lower a person's stress hormone levels. Making a point to spend some time in nature will help your physical and mental health. The following are some great ways to get out in nature:

- Horseback riding
- Go paddle-boarding
- Go to a farm and pick berries
- Walk around a botanical garden
- Sit under a tree
- Hike to a waterfall
- Walk around a lake

There are numerous things that you can do in nature. Basically, you just need to get out and enjoy it.

Chapter 3:
SLEEP DISORDERS

Insomnia is probably one of the most common sleep disorders. It is characterized by the inability to fall asleep, stay asleep, waking up too early, or requiring medication to get to sleep. Put, with insomnia, and you don't sleep well. CBT-I is a special form of cognitive-behavioral therapy that focuses on improving sleep quality. It is designed for people who need help working through their insomnia or other sleep issues.

It's also important to make sure that some other health problem is not causing your insomnia. Insomnia is a common side effect of prescription medication and other mental health problems, like anxiety, depression, or psychological stress. While these techniques could still help you, they may need to be adjusted to fit whatever may be causing your problems.

Make sure that you use a variety of these techniques every single day for six to eight weeks. If CBT-I works for you, you should start to see improvement in your sleep during this time. If you have been struggling with insomnia for some time, it is going to take a while to rewire your brain to be a night of good sleep, so you can't expect these techniques to work the very first night. Six weeks is typically the fastest you can become skilled at these techniques, so don't rush the process.

Some of the most common forms of CBT that are used to treat sleep disorders include:

- Stimulus Control

A stimulus is anything that will create a response within you. This technique aims to make sure you have a positive response to your bed at night. This is commonly used for people who tend to toss and turn, unable to go to sleep. When this constantly occurs for several nights, you start to get frustrated. This can end up causing you to dread bedtime, expecting that you are going to toss and turn for hours. Bedtime and your bed will create a negative response with you.

This will teach you to use the bed for only sleep and sex. You shouldn't watch TV, read, or do anything else while in bed. You also learn that you should only go to bed once you are very sleepy. If you don't go to sleep within 20 minutes, then get out of bed to something to help you relax. Once you feel sleepy again, go back to bed. With time, this will help you to fall asleep more quickly once you get into your bed. Your response to the bed and bedtime will become positive.

- Sleep Restriction

This will set strict limits on the amount of time that you spend in bed every night. The starting limit will typically be the same as how much sleep you normally get each night. For example, you might only get five good hours of sleep even though you are spending seven hours in bed. In this case, you would have an initial limit of five hours in bed. This means that you are going to be likely to get less than five hours of sleep.

This sleep loss will make you even more tire, but it is also going to help you get to sleep faster and wake up less often during the night. This will help to give you a solid period of sleep and a stable sleep pattern. As you see improvements in your sleep, your limit will slowly be increased.

- Biofeedback and Relaxation Training

Relaxation training helps you learn how to calm your mind and body and help relieve tension and anxiety. Biofeedback is used along with this. This process will involve your brain, breathing, heart, and muscles. Biofeedback will teach you how to raise and lower different signs of how your body is functioning.

To improve your sleep, you are taught how to change your brain waves or muscle tension. You have to wear a device that tells you your brain wave frequency or muscle tension level. You will then try to change it so that you can get to sleep.

- Psychotherapy and Cognitive Control

This will help you to identify beliefs and attitudes that could be keeping you from sleeping well. These negative thoughts tend to involve stress and worries. You will learn how to overcome these negative thoughts.

- Sleep Hygiene

This method will help correct the things that you do every day that could affect your sleep. Sleep hygiene is made up of basic tips and habits that can help you create a healthy sleep pattern. Disturbed sleep is most often caused by more than one thing.

Sleep Diary

The first thing you need to start doing is keeping a sleep diary. This can help you to spot problem areas where you need to work on things. To create your sleep diary, all you need to do is create a chart on a piece of paper. Across the top, write out the days of the week. Down the left side of the chart, list the following:

- Naps – each day, you will write down the number of naps you took.
- Bedtime – each day, write down what time you got into bed.
- Fall Asleep Time – put down what time you actually fell asleep.

- Times Awake Overnight – write down the number of times you woke up that night.
- Wake Up Time – write down what time you got up in the morning.
- Got Out of Bed Time – write down the time you actually got out of the bed.
- Total Time Asleep – write down the amount of time you actually slept.
- Total Time in Bed – write down the amount of time you spent in the bed, including sleep.
- Calculated Sleep Efficiency – divide the amount of time spent asleep in minutes by the amount of time you spent in bed minutes.
- Did you follow sleep stimulus control guidelines?
- Did you use relaxation if needed?
- POSITIVE sleep thought

Some of this may be hard to figure out but do your best. If you have a smartwatch like an Apple or FitBit, they can help you keep track of your sleep and fill out your sleep diary.

Progressive Muscle Relaxation

Having negative thoughts about your insomnia will only make the problem worse. You have to make sure you can stop those negative thoughts and make them positive. This can be difficult to do. Stress is commonly linked to muscle tension. A progressive muscle relaxation exercise can help to calm the mind and body. This exercise can help you to fall asleep.

As you lay in bed, you will work through your body from foot to head, tensing and relaxing all of the muscles. Do so in the following order:

1. Right Foot – tense the foot by curling the toes, and hold until you can't anymore and release.
2. Left Foot and Right Foot – tense both feet by curling the toes, holding until you can't anymore.
3. Both Feet and Right Calf – repeat the tensing and releasing process.
4. Both Feet and Both Calves
5. Previous muscle groups, plus a right upper leg
6. Add in the left upper leg
7. Add in the buttocks – now you are tensing the entire lower body
8. Feet, legs, buttocks, and the low back – make sure that you don't hurt your back while doing this.
9. All previous muscle groups, plus mid-back
10. All previous muscle groups, plus upper back
11. Add in the shoulders
12. All previous muscle groups, plus the right hand

13. Add the left hand

14. All previous muscle groups, plus the entire right arm

15. Add the left arm

16. Add in the chest

17. Entire lower body, entire upper body, plus the neck

18. All previous muscle groups, plus the face

19. The entire body at the same time

This process should take about five to ten minutes. You can also play relaxation music during this time.

Stimulus Control

As mentioned earlier, you want your bed and bedroom to trigger you to feel positive about sleep. With insomnia, that association is likely negative. The following rules will help you to change the stimulus of your bed and bedroom.

1. Go to bed and lay down in your bed only when you are feeling sleepy.

2. When you are in bed, do not read or watch television.

3. Once you are in bed, if you find that you can't fall asleep within 20 minutes, get up and go into a different room. Stay up as long as you have to and go back to your bed once you feel sleepy again.

4. If you are still unable to fall asleep, repeat step three. Do this as often as you have to during the night.

It might be hard to get out of bed when all you want to be doing is sleeping, but the goal is to work for several weeks to change the connections you have created in your brain to help you become a better sleeper.

Sleep Restriction

While it sounds counterintuitive, restricting the amount of sleep you get each night can help you to sleep more. Make sure that during this process, you do not restrict your sleep to less than five hours. Sleep restriction may not be a good technique to use if you have chronic pain, seizure disorder, bipolar disorder, or other health conditions.

First, let's cover sleep efficiency. You should be filling out that section on your sleep diary. Sleep efficiency shows the amount of time you were asleep versus how much time you spend in bed. Ideally, you want your sleep efficiency to be around 85%. This is figured out by diving time asleep by time in bed and then multiplying by 100 to get the percentage.

Let's say you filled out your sleep diary as such:

Bedtime – 10 PM

Fell Asleep – 11 PM

Awake – 2 AM to 3 AM

Woke Up – 7 AM

Out of Bed – 8 AM

You spend ten hours in bed and seven hours asleep. That would place your sleep efficiency at 70%. Here is how to do sleep restriction to improve that number.

1. Keep up with a sleep diary for two weeks.
2. Set a wake-up time based on when you need to get up for the day and ensure that you keep that the same every day.
3. Figure out the average of the total time you spend in bed each night from your sleep diary.
4. Restrict your time in bed to that average number. You would count back from your wake-up time to see when you would get into bed. That means if you need to get up by eight and your restricted number is 7, then you would go to be at 1 AM.
5. Continue to keep your sleep diary. Stay with the restricted time until you reach a sleep efficiency score of 90% or more
6. Once you reach that number, increase your time in bed by 15 minutes. This means if your bedtime was 1 AM, it would now be 12:45 AM.
7. Don't change this for five days. If you stick with a 90% efficiency rating, add another 15 minutes for the next five days.
8. If your sleep efficiency is between 85 and 90 percent, don't change how much time you spend in bed.

9. If the efficiency drops below 85%, then decrease the time you spend in bed by 15 minutes.

Continue this process until you figure out the best amount of time for you to spend in bed sleeping so that you are well-rested. This could be seven hours, so that you would keep your time in bed set to seven hours. However, you could find that you do better when you get nine hours.

Chapter 4:
MOOD DISORDERS

CBT is most well known for its ability to help with various mood disorders. CBT can help treat mild to moderate depression, anxiety, and other mood disorders just as well, if not better, than medication. It can also help severe cases, but it is best to be under a highly skilled therapist's supervision. CBT can also be combined with other treatments, like antidepressants and other types of drugs.

CBT helps you spot the negative thoughts that are affecting your mood and then teach you how to swap those out for positive ones. This change in attitude will create a change in your actions. This can, in turn, relieve symptoms of depression, anxiety, and so on.

If you find that you wake up each morning thinking, "What's the point in trying?" CBT can teach you to tell yourself, "That thought isn't helpful. Making an effort has lots of rewards. I'll start by getting out of bed."

CBT for anxiety is much more effective than medication due to the simple fact that anti-anxiety medication tends to be addictive and only treats the symptom. CBT and therapy can help you to uncover the underlying causes of your fears and worries. It can also help you relax, look at situations in a new light, and develop better coping skills.

When it comes to bipolar disorder, CBT can help you regularize your sleep, as spending too much time in bed will often trigger a depressive episode, or too much can trigger mania. It can also help identify impulsivity and hyper-positive thinking that can plague your thinking. CBT can help you to delay gratification, slow down, maintain awareness, plan activities, distance yourself from the tug of mania, and be more conscious of how their actions can affect them.

Anxiety Coping Skills

Anxiety is characterized by intense worry and can also be accompanied by panic attacks. There are certain coping skills that you can use that can help you to calm your mind and body and help you to start thinking straight again.

1. Deep Breathing

Deep breathing is a simple exercise that can help you to manage emotions. Not only is deep breathing helpful, but it is also easy and discreet so that you can do it anywhere and at any time.

To practice deep breathing, sit in a comfortable position and place your hand on your stomach. Take a deep breath in through your nose so that you can feel your hand on your stomach rise. Hold that breath in your lungs, and then slowly release the breath through your mouth, with your lips puckers as if you were breathing through a straw. To help make your deep breathing more effective, go slowly. Count to four as you breathe in, how for four seconds, and then breath out to a count of six.

2. Progressive Muscle Relaxation

Through the act of tensing and relaxing your muscles, you can reach a powerful feeling of relaxation. Plus, this technique can help you spot where anxiety is located by showing you how to spot your tension feelings.

You should start out by getting into a comfortable seated or reclined position; for the various areas listed below, tense that muscle up as tight as you can, but not so hard that you strain it. Hold this for ten seconds, noticing how it feels. Then, release that tension and notice how that relaxation feels compared to the feeling of tension.

- Feet – Curl your toes into your feet and release.
- Calves – Flex or point your feet, and then relax.

- Thighs – Squeeze your things tightly together, and release.
- Torso – Suck your stomach in, and then release the tension.
- Back – Squeeze your shoulder blades together, and release
- Shoulders – Lift and squeeze your shoulders up to your ears, and then let them drop.
- Arms – Make fists and squeeze them up to your shoulders, and then release.
- Hands – Make a fist, and then relax.
- Face – Scrunch up your face, and then relax.
- Full Body – Squeeze all of the muscle groups at once, and then release.

3. Challenging Irrational Thoughts

Anxiety does a great job at magnifying irrational thoughts. For example, something like "I will make a mistake" or "something bad is going to happen" might lack evidence, but it will still impact how you feel. When you examine the evidence and challenge those thoughts, it can reduce your anxiety.

One way to do this is to put your thoughts on trail. Pick a thought that has caused you anxiety. Gather up as much information as you can in support of the thought. These need to be verifiable facts only, and then gather information against your thought. Compare your evidence and figure out if your thought is accurate or not.

Another option is Socratic questioning. The question you thought by asking yourself things like:

- "Is my thought based on feeling or fact?"
- "How would my best friend see this situation?"
- "How likely is it that my fear will come true?"
- "What's most likely to happen?"
- "If my fear comes true, is it going to matter a week, month, or year down the road?"

4. Imagery

Thoughts can help you change how you feel. If you think of something sad, there is a good chance you will start to feel sad. The opposite is also true. You can think of something happy and begin to feel happy.

Think about a place that you find comforting. This may be a quiet mountaintop, your bedroom, a secluded beach, or even a concert. For about five to ten minutes, use every sense to imagine this in as much detail as you can. You need to really imagine this place. What things can you see? What things can you hear? What can you taste? Are you eating or drinking something. What can you feel? What is the temperature like? What can you smell?

Decastastrophizing

Cognitive distortions are types of irrational thoughts that can end up influencing how you feel. Everybody will have some sort of cognitive distortion. They are completely normal. However, when these distortions become too extreme, or you have too many, they can hurt you.

One of the most common forms of cognitive distortion is known as catastrophizing. When you catastrophize, you exaggerate the importance of a problem or think up the worst possible outcome by learning how to questions your thoughts; you can then correct these distortions. The next time you experience catastrophizing, answer the following.

What are you currently worried about?

_____

_____

_____

What are the chances that your worry is going to come true? Write down some examples of past experiences or some type of evidence that supports your answer.

_____

_____

_____

If your worry were to come true, what is the absolute worst thing that could happen?

_____

_____

_____

If your worry were to come true, what is the most likely thing that will happen?

_____

_____

_____

If your worry does come true, what are the chances you will be okay:

- In one week? _____%

- In one month? _____%

- In one year? _____%

Bipolar Disorder Warning Signs

To manage your bipolar disorder, you will want to learn about your warning signs. These are little clues that you are going to tip you off and let you know if you are getting ready to experience a manic or depressive episode. If you can spot an oncoming episode before it fully takes you over, you can prepare, get help, and minimize the damage.

To figure out your warning signs, answer the following questions for your depression warning signs and your mania warning signs.

How do your feelings change?

Depression:

_____

_____

_____

Mania

___

___

___

How do your thoughts change?

Depression:

___

___

___

Mania:

___

___

___

How do you behave differently?

Depression:

___

___

___

Mania:

___

___

___

Do you notice any other changes?

Depression:

___

___

___

Mania:

___

Challenging Anxious Thoughts

Anxiety, at times, can be healthy. It's healthy when it forces you to focus on your problems and to work on solving them. But it can grow out of control, and that is when it does the opposite. It can cripple our ability to fix problems. When this starts to happen, irrational thoughts tend to play big roles.

In this exercise, you will learn how to catch your irrational thoughts and then replace them with rational ones. With enough practice, this will become second nature and can help you manage your anxiety

Describe a situation that often triggers your anxiety.

___

Anxiety will distort our thinking by causing us to overestimate the chances that something is going to go wrong and imagine the possible consequences as way worse than they actually are. Sometimes, take a few minutes to think about these things can help us spot those irrational thoughts.

Imagine that you have to face an anxiety-producing situation like what you listed above. Describe the...

Worst outcome:

___

Best Outcome:

___

Likely Outcome:

___

Imagine if the worst outcome ends up coming true. Is it still going to matter...

One week from now:

___

One month from now:

_____

One year from now:

_____

Usually, your anxious thoughts will focus on the worst outcome, even if that isn't likely to happen. For example, a person who is afraid to give a speech could think, "I am going to forget what I have to say and will embarrass myself, and never live it down."

As an observer, we know that a more rational alternative to that thought would be, "My speech might only be okay, but if I mess up, everybody is going to forget about it."

Using your worst outcome and likely outcome from above, describe your…

Irrational thought:

_____

Rational thought:

_____

Positive Journal

Every day will bring about a combo of bad and good experiences. Unfortunately, our brains tend to focus more on the bad experiences while discounting all of the good things that happened. For example, we are more likely to remember that single awkward interaction over the hundreds of normal interactions we had.

For this exercise, all you have to do is write down at least three positive experiences you have every single day. These things can be tiny, but they will help to improve your mood.

Chapter 5: ADHD

There is a lot of interest and confusion about CBT and its use to help adults who have ADHD. CBT focuses on behaviors and thoughts that happen during our day. This is a different approach than the normal type of psychodynamic and psychoanalytic therapy. These involve reprocessing and recapturing childhood experiences that have causes emotional problems. One difference with CBT is that it is goal-oriented, and the methods used will be clearly stated and has to be measured for every person.

How CBT Helps Adults Who Have ADHD

CBT can help adults who have ADHD in several ways. First, CBT has been developed especially for adults who have ADHD. Some programs try to help adults overcome the hardships with the executive functions of their lives that they need to manage their time, organize and then plan out long term goals. The other will focus on regulating emotions, stress management, and controlling impulses.

It has been established that adults who have ADHD suffer from depressive and anxiety disorders. A huge study found that about 51 percent of adults who have ADHD suffered from anxiety, and around 32 percent suffered from depression. Because of this, CBT can be very helpful to adults who have ADHD, although they haven't been designed primarily to address the impairments and symptoms associated with ADHD.

Therapy that addresses executive dysfunction falls into this category since they use more adaptive cognitions about ways to go about organizing, planning, etc. It also imparts more behavioral skills. One example of adaptive cognition is instructing yourself to "break down unpleasant or complex tasks into more manageable pieces." Some examples of behavioral skills could be implementing a filing system or using a daily planner. Positive behaviors and thoughts can reinforce each other. As a person gets better at managing their time, they will have more cognitions and beliefs about themselves. These will help them maintain and generate better behaviors.

CBT and Medications

Both non-stimulant and stimulant medications have been studied in treating ADHD in adults. The research they have done so far shows CBT can benefit whether the person is or isn't taking any medications. There haven't been any direct comparisons between drugs and CBT. Still, clinical experiences suggest they have various effects: Even though medicine can help control the main symptoms of distractibility, impulsivity, and short attention spans, CBT is better at increasing the skills and habits that are needed for self-management. It could also help to improve interpersonal and emotional regulation.

ADHD Focus Plan

Adults who have ADHD might find it hard to focus on important tasks. It can cause them to feel overwhelmed, get distracted, procrastinate, or just forget about it entirely. CBT can teach them practical skills that will address these problems.

This exercise combines practical skills into a simple planning process. Patients will pick a task that they have to finish, break it down into smaller pieces, and then schedule the times to give their full attention to the task. Last, they will visualize all the benefits they will be getting once they finish the task. This will counteract their tendency to focus on the task processes, which could be undesirable or hard, as opposed to all the positive outcomes.

This exercise is a great way to introduce a patient to basic time management and organizational skills. With some practice, clients could choose to "graduate" from this exercise to a simple planner entry covering the main points in a better format.

1. Define The Task

Write down one task that you need to finish this week. For example: "clean the house because my parents are coming."

_____

_____

_____

2. Break The Task Into Smaller Pieces

When you break a large task into smaller ones, it makes it feel like it is more manageable. "Clean the house" could sound like too much of a task to undertake but "washing the dishes" or "doing the laundry" is a lot easier to handle. Make two columns, and on the left-hand side, write all the parts of the task, and on the right-hand side, write how much time it will take you to do each job.

_____

_____

_____

3. Make A Schedule

Give the task a certain time or add it into a normal daily activity like: "put a load of laundry in the washer when I get home from work." Plan out the way you will remember to do this task like: "put a reminder into my phone."

_____

_____

_____

4. Get Ready For The Task

You need to list out the ways you need to get ready to do the task before its scheduled time.

- Get Rid of Distractions: List all the distractions that you need to get rid of before you begin the task, like turning off the television or putting your phone on silence.

_____

_____

_____

- Plan for Distractions That You Can't Avoid

Make some "if" and "then" plans for distractions that might happen like "If my friend calls, then I will tell them that I will call them back in ten minutes."

_____

_____

_____

- Supplies and Materials

List all the items you are going to need to finish the task at hand, like laundry detergent, sponges, dish soap, etc.

_____

_____

_____

- Physically Getting Prepared

Write down all the actions that you need to take to be ready for the task, like eating a snack, getting home on time, or dressing appropriately.

_____

_____

_____

5. Visualize the Outcome

Most people don't think about all the positive feelings that can come from finishing a task you have been procrastinating about. List all the benefits of finishing the task and the way you will feel because of it.

_____

_____

_____

Managing ADHD

ADHD isn't just about having problems at work; it could also contribute to lesser self-esteem, problems within a romantic relationship, and possibly car accidents. The good news is that a "little bit can go a long way" when treating ADHD. For some people, just being aware of their weaknesses and creating strategies that counter them could result in large improvements.

The exercise below describes five skills that can help people who have ADHD. These skills might include: living a healthy lifestyle, creating a good environment, getting and staying organized, setting aside some time for your relationships, and creating structure. Every section will describe how important the skill is and some tips for using it successfully.

Let me emphasize that this exercise has lots of content. This can be a bit overwhelming if you try to do too much of it at one time. Try to pick one or two sections and focus on them for one hour.

Even though there isn't a cure for ADHD, some people find that they can manage their symptoms with some hard work and practice. Being diagnosed with ADHD isn't the end of the world. It doesn't make you a bad partner or mean that you can't have a good career. Your path to achieve these goals could be different from another person.

Below you will find some solutions to the challenges you might be facing with ADHD. You can use this tool as a beginning point to think about the areas you want to grow in and then start making solutions to those problems.

Creating Structure

The symptoms of ADHD could be tamed down by having a routine and some structure. If we don't have structure, our daily obligations might get overwhelming and jumbled, or we just might forget about them. Having a routine can help you focus on just one single thing without any room for distractions.

You have to set aside time for every single thing. Try to make a habit of eating, sleeping, working, and relaxing at the same exact time each day. This can help you follow through with all of your daily tasks. It might be a bit hard to keep this routine initially, but with some time and practice, you will get into a groove, and it will be second nature to you.

- Never be too ambitious: Having a realistic routine is a lot better than having a perfect one. Look at this example: setting aside 30-minute study sessions might be more productive than trying to power through a three-hour session.
- Prioritize large tasks like working, meals, and sleep. These are known as "anchors." The remainder of your day revolves around them. Add smaller tasks to these anchors like "I will take a walk after I eat dinner."
- Many people worry that having a structured day is going to be boring. The fact is, it is only boring if you make it boring. Add

some fun activities into your daily routine and set some time aside so you can still be spontaneous.

- When you are just beginning this new way of life, write down everything and set alarms. Remember to set your alarms a couple of minutes earlier so that you will have the time to get ready for every task.

Set Time Aside for Your Relationships
There might be times when your ADHD symptoms can make you seem uncaring and indifferent, even if it isn't the case. It might be hard for some people not to interrupt others, to sit still while listening without finding other things to do. You might forget an anniversary or birthday because you have been juggling a lot of responsibilities. It doesn't matter what you are struggling with, and you have to set aside some time for your relationship.

If you have problems focusing on your partner after a long day at work, schedule some short time periods when you won't do anything but listen to them. This time doesn't need to be any longer than ten minutes. Set a timer and put your phone away. Give your partner 100 percent of your attention. Having a good ten minutes is a lot better than having 20 bad minutes. But your partner must agree with you on this. If they aren't on board, you are going to be sitting there talking to yourself.

For some couples, not having enough understanding is a huge problem. Take some time to talk to your partner about your ADHD and ask them to do some research about the condition so they can understand you better. Some therapists are willing to meet your partner to answer any questions they might have, give you some education, and help cover the gap.

Don't forget to keep your relationship with the people you don't see each day. Make reminders for other special occasions, too. Schedule some phone calls to family and friends.

Remain Organized

Clutter is ADHD's enemy. While you move from one task to another, projects that you haven't finished can take over your mental and physical space. This can lead to distractions and a possibility that you will either forget or lose something.

- Make to-do lists. Begin with the easiest and fastest items so that you will be able to see some quick progress.

- Make sure your workspace stays clean. Get everything off of your desk except what you are working on right this minute. Plus, give yourself an extra five minutes in the end to get your desk organized for the next day.

- Get rid of old papers, clothes, knick-knacks, or other things that you don't need around your office or home. If you have been hanging on to things for five years just because "you might need it," it is time to get rid of it.

- If a task pops up that is only going to take you 30 seconds to do, and you aren't in the middle of something important, do it immediately. Now, you can mark it off of your to-do list.

Create An Environment That Is Yours

What are some things that help you to concentrate? What causes you to lose focus when you are working? People who have ADHD need lots of stimuli. They normally work better in places where it is loud and vibrant. Other people need just the opposite, no phones, no televisions, no sounds, just the task at hand. Find all the things you need and make an environment that suits you.

- If You Need Activity and Noise
    - Schedule regular breaks to take a walk. Set a timer while you are walking so that you know when you need to go back to work.
    - If your office is boring, try hanging up some pictures you like that will liven it up. Add colors, photos, and anything else that stimulates you.
    - Listen to music, turn the television up louder or tune it to something that interests you.

- If You Need Quiet
    - Turn off the television, close the door, closeout emails. Limit all pesky distractions that seem to pop up when you are working.
    - Designate an area in your home for your office, even if it is only a little corner, and then eliminate all distractions.
    - If your office is noisy, use noise-canceling headphones to get rid of all the background noises.

- Healthy Lifestyle

Sleep, nutrition, and exercise without these things, you will have a very hard time getting control over your ADHD, and it won't matter what steps you try to take. Even a person who doesn't have ADHD will get restless if they don't get any exercise. They remain distracted without sleep or food. All the detrimental effects get magnified by your ADHD.

Find an exercise you enjoy doing. Even walking for 30 minutes could have a good impact on your health. If you like participating in sports, they are a good outlet if you like adrenaline rushes.

Sleeping is different for everyone. Eight hours each night is normally enough for normal people, but some people need more, and some might not need as much. Get into a steady routine and stick with it even on the weekends.

The information about what good nutrition does for ADHD isn't all that clear, but most people believe a high protein diet while being low in sugars could help. It is important to make sure you eat several meals throughout your well balanced day. Planned meals can double as a good way to keep your routine.

Chapter 6: ANGER

Anger is one of the more extreme emotions that humans can experience. When we have healthy ways of managing our anger, it helps us maintain healthy boundaries and achieve more. When we can't control our anger, it turns destructive and can cause unnecessary harm and pain to ourselves and others. CBT can help people get a better grip on their anger and channel it into something that is positive.

Some of the most common benefits of using CBT for anger are:

- Learn how natural anger response can be expressed healthily.
- Learn different anger management techniques that will help you express yourself assertively and maintain control.
- Learn the positive power of anger and how to use it to improve your wellbeing and relationships.

- Replace unhelpful angry actions with helpful forms of communications.
- Learn how to lower the overwhelming triggers that cause an angry reaction.
- Discover the main cause of your anger, which unnecessarily fuels the intensity of the anger.

Using these CBT techniques, you finally find that you understand your triggers more and prevent angry outbursts. Once you have a good understanding of triggers and your anger's root cause, you can start to learn which techniques work best to soothe your anger.

Triggers

A trigger is a stimulus, like a thing, person, situation, or place, that causes an unwanted behavioral or emotional response.

The Problem: Describe the problem that your triggers are adding to. What is the worst thing that can happen if you become exposed to a trigger?

_____

_____

_____

Trigger Categories: Nearly anything has the chance to become a trigger. To start exploring your trigger, think about the following categories. Is there are certain emotion that acts as a trigger? How about a place or a person? List out your responses.

Emotional State:

_____

_____

_____

People:

_____

_____

_____

Places:

_____

_____

_____

Things:

_____

_____

_____

Thoughts:

_____

_____

_____

Activities/Situations:

_____

_____

_____

Now that you have an idea of your triggers, we will go over coming up with a plan to deal with your three biggest triggers. Review your plan regularly, and make sure you practice it.

Describe Your Three Main Triggers

Use plenty of details to describe what your three biggest triggers are.

_____

_____

_____

Describe a Way to Avoid or Reduce Exposure to the Trigger

_____

_____

_____

Describe a Strategy for Dealing with Each Trigger Face On, When You Can't Avoid It

_____

_____

_____

When Anger Becomes a Problem

In small doses, anger is a healthy, appropriate, and normal emotion. Everyone will experience anger at some point. It allows us to stand up for ourselves when somebody has wronged us and protects our needs. However, there are many times when anger can have negative consequences. Below, we will go over some examples of how anger can become harmful.

Anger becomes a problem when it starts to affect others negatively. Anger causes a person to want to act in a harmful or unpleasant way to people around us. This can cause us to strain or lose important relationships. It can be hard to maintain a healthy relationship when anger becomes out of control.

Going by the above statement of your anger negatively affecting others, how much does that apply to you?

- Not at all
- A little
- Somewhat
- Very much

In what ways has your anger impacted others?

_____

_____

_____

Anger becomes a problem when it prevents you from performing well at school or work. Anger can cause breakdowns in communication, making it hard to work with others. Plus, being preoccupied with your anger can harm your ability to concentrate on your task.

How much does this statement apply to you?

- Not at all
- A little
- Somewhat
- Very much

In what ways has your anger negatively affected your performance at school or work?

_____

_____

_____

Anger becomes a problem when it has a negative impact on your wellbeing or health. Anger can affect your emotional and physical health. Physically, anger will contribute to problems like heart attacks and high blood pressure. Emotionally, anger can cause drug and alcohol use, anxiety, and depression.

How much does that statement apply to you?

- Not at all
- A little
- Somewhat
- Very much

In what ways has your anger negatively impacted your emotional or physical health?

_____

_____

_____

Anger becomes a problem when it's too intense. Even when your anger is justified, it can be an issue if it goes too far. For example, physical aggression can cause serious consequences, like physical harm to yourself or others, legal troubles, or property damage. A verbal outburst that is disproportionate to a situation can cause you to lose your job, permanently harm a relationship, or other severe consequences.

How much does that statement apply to you?

- Not at all
- A little
- Somewhat
- Very much

When was the last time that you experienced extreme anger?

_____

_____

_____

Coping Skills

The first coping skill for anger is to be aware of your triggers. Triggers are what set you off, and knowing them, and being cautious when you are around them, will reduce the chances that your anger will get out of control.

How you can use your triggers to help you:

1. Come up with a list of all of your triggers and read over them each day. Reviewing your triggers keeps them in mind, increasing the chance you will notice them before they cause a problem.

2. Often, the best way to handle a trigger is to make sure you avoid it. This could mean making changes in your routine, life, or relationships.

3. Because you can't always avoid triggers, having a plan for when you do face them helps. For example, avoid touchy conversations when you are feeling upset, tired, or hungry.

Next, you can practice deep breathing.

Deep breathing is one of the most simple techniques that can help you to manage your emotions. Not only is it effective, but it's discreet, and you can do it no matter where you are.

To perform deep breathing, sit in a comfortable position and place a hand on your stomach. Take a deep breath in through your nose for a count of four, feeling your hand rise. Hold this breath at the top for a count of four. Then release the breath through your mouth for a count of six, feeling your hand fall.

It would help if you also kept an anger log.

After you have experienced anger, take some time to record what your experience was like. This will help you spot patterns, triggers, and warning signs while also keeping your thoughts organized.

1. What occurred before you felt angry? Describe how you felt and what was going through your mind. Were you stressed, hungry, or tired?
2. Describe exactly what happened. What event triggered this? How did you respond, and did your reaction change as things continued?
3. What feelings and thoughts did you have during your episode? Looking back, do you see things differently than you did in the heat of the moment?

You can also use diversions.

The goal of using diversions is to give yourself some time. If you can distract yourself for only 30 minutes, you will have a better chance of facing your anger healthily. You can also go back to your source of anger later on. You are simply setting the problem aside for now. Different diversions include:

- Rearrange a room
- Play with your pet
- Take pictures
- Go on a hike
- Play an instrument
- Call a friend
- Workout
- Play a game
- Write
- Take a bath
- Cook
- Do a craft
- Do yard work
- Clean
- Listen to music
- Go for a walk

- Read
- Watch a movie

You can also give yourself a time-out.

Time-outs are a great tool for relationships where anger-fueled disagreements are creating issues. When a person calls a time-out, both people agree to take a step away from the issue and return once you have both cooled off.

1. You and your partner need to plan out exactly the way the time-outs will work. Everybody needs to understand the rationale of the time-out. Meaning, you want to cool down and avoid the issue.

2. What will you do during the time-out? Plan something in different places. The diversions list above is a great place to start

3. Plan to come back to the issue at hand in 20 minutes to an hour. Important problems should never be ignored completely, but nothing good will happen from an explosive argument.

Lastly, it's important to know the warning signs of anger. Your body will clue you in as to when you are experiencing anger. The most common warning signs are:

- You go quiet or shut
- Upset stomach
- Aggressive body language

- Pacing
- The use of verbal insults
- Raised voice
- Becoming argumentative
- Headaches
- Clenched fists
- Feel hot or turn red
- Can't let go of the problem
- Sweating

Chapter 7:
OCD

OCD, or obsessive-compulsive disorder, is likely one of the most popular things to say you have without truly suffering from it at all. It is widespread to hear a person say, "I'm so OCD!" when referring to the fact that they like to have things a certain way. However, to actually have OCD, you are going to have much more serious symptoms. OCD is frustrating and scary, and by definition, it is impairing and time-consuming. Just because you like to keep a clean house does not mean you have OCD.

OCD requires two things, obsessions and compulsions. Obsessions are characterized by images, urges, or thoughts that you can't shake. They are unwanted and intrusive, and they cause you to start feeling anxiety, doubt, and shame. Some of the most common obsessions are:

- Fear of harming others or self
- Concern about morality or upsetting God
- Excessive concern about exactness or evenness
- Fear of losing control
- Unwanted violent or sexual thoughts
- Fear of contamination

Compulsions are characterized by repetitive actions that person feels they have to perform and are often in response to obsessions. People perform their compulsions hoping that they will get rid of the anxiety. Common compulsions are:

- Excessively check that you didn't make a mistake
- Mentally going over something again and again
- Rearranging things until it feels right
- Repeating certain activities a specific number of times
- Mentally reassuring yourself that everything is okay
- Washing or cleaning excessively

During treatment, that cycle has to be found and broken. One type of treatment is exposure therapy. Like those based on insights and finding the root cause, some types of psychotherapy can create more harm than good when dealing with OCD. All this does is place more focus on their compulsions and obsessions without helping them manage them.

When it comes to exposure therapy, you are exposed to the things that cause you anxiety, and then you learn how to refrain from your compulsive actions. This helps to break the cycle without causing any undue stress.

Before you start your exposure therapy, you need to identify your specific obsession, compulsions, and anxiety sources. This is going to require some self-exploration. Try focusing on things that you try to avoid. The exposure hierarchy that you will be going through next will act as a roadmap. You will take those things and work from the least difficult to most difficult to help get rid of your obsessions and compulsions.

If your OCD is extreme, and the tiniest thing causes a trigger, this process should be done for the therapists' safety. There they can help you come up with a narrative about exposure to your trigger. This means that you won't have to face the trigger physically, but the story will still trigger you to work on not performing your compulsion. This is the safest way to work your way up to actually facing the trigger. Imagination is only one step towards working through your therapy.

Suppose you have a mental compulsion as opposed to a physical one, such as internal counting, prayers, self-reassurance, and so on. In that case, it can be a bit more challenging to control during your exposure therapy. These compulsions tend to be automatic and nearly involuntary.

One of the first things you can try is to distract yourself, but this is only a form of avoidance and won't get rid of the problem. Instead, you are going to have to learn how to spoil your mental compulsions by being exposed to what triggers your thoughts.

For example, if conversations cause you a lot of anxiety, Afterwards, you may want to mentally review the conversation, trying to find evidence that you acted normally. You can spoil this process by replacing your compulsory thoughts with an alternative, like "I might have made a fool of myself during the conversation."

Exposure Hierarchy for OCD

What you need to do is come up with a list of anxiety-causing situations, starting with the most distressing and ending with the least. Then go through and rank each on a scale of one to ten, with one being not distressing at all and ten being the most distressing.

_____

_____

_____

Once you have done that, you are going to start purposefully exposing yourself to these distressing situations. Starting at the bottom of your list, with the least distressing things, pick a situation you want to practice for a week. Write that down:

_____

_____

_____

You will want to try to make sure you experience that thing at least once a day for an entire week. You have to refrain from any compulsion you want to do once you are exposed to the obsession for at least two hours. Each day, rate how hard it was to complete that exercise. Use a scale of one to ten, with one being very easy to do and ten being very difficult. Rate it for each day below.

- Monday
- Tuesday
- Wednesday
- Thursday
- Friday
- Saturday
- Sunday

At the end of the week, take a moment to write out anything that you learned while doing this.

_____

_____

_____

If you feel you need to continue working on this distressing situation, go another week working with this one. If you feel you have worked through your fear of this situation, you can move onto the next distressing situation. Your anxiety about something does not have to be at zero before moving onto something else, but you want to make sure that the next task feels manageable while still be challenging.

Chapter 8:
EATING DISORDERS

Let's start this off with an example. A woman, we'll call her Amanda, has an eating disorder. She is preoccupied with the idea that she is fat and that everybody is judging her because of that. This is such a problem that she refuses to take any sort of public transportation because she is afraid the people will make fun of her weight. This idea that she is horribly overweight has caused her to become bulimic.

With CBT, we view people's emotional state due to how they interpret or think about a situation and not as an inevitable result of something. Let's look at Amanda not wanting to take the bus.

Since she is preoccupied with her weight and looks, it's not unusual that she assumes others have the same preoccupation. She may board the bus and notice that somebody looks at her. Her initial thought is going to be, "That person thinks I'm fat and that I shouldn't be in public." This reinforces her idea that she is fat and needs to lose weight and make her feel bad.

However, if you put a different person in that situation, they may conclude that the person looking at them admires them. If Amanda had this thought process, she wouldn't feel bad at all.

So, we do not have two identical situations that have ended in each person feeling differently in the end. Each person has tried to explain, understand, and interpret the reason a person on the bus has looked at them. Still, both are very different thoughts about the situation.

These are what are known as automatic thoughts. They happen very quickly. They can be helpful and give us a chance to evaluate a situation quickly, but sometimes they are unrealistic and negative. If thoughts are often self-critical, it's not that hard to understand why a person could end up feeling depressed due to their thoughts.

CBT has a larger amount of research done on it than any other psychotherapy when treating eating disorders. This is especially true when it comes to bulimia nervosa.

When you first start using CBT for eating disorders, the goal is to start keeping a journal of your eating habits and thoughts, as well as different situations that caused you to feel a certain way. This will increase your awareness that eating-disordered actions have taken place when certain feelings or thoughts come up. This helps you to remove yourself from autopilot and retake control of your eating habits.

It's essential to slowly go at this because simply distinguishing from thought and feeling can be hard to do. It can also be helpful to learn the difference between emotions, particularly hurt and anger. Aside from starting a food journal, let's look at some other important CBT activities that you should do.

Self-Care Assessment

Self-care is anything that you do to maintain good health and to help your overall wellbeing. You may find that some of the things below are already part of your normal routine. However, you may find some things you don't do or do too much of. In this assessment, you need to think about how frequently or how well you are doing these different self-care activities. The goal is to learn about your own self-care needs by seeing the areas in which you need to pay more attention.

There are no right or wrong answers to this assessment, but you must fill it out truthfully. If you aren't sure, you can ask others how they think you do in some of these categories, but it's best if you really do some self-exploration and answer them on your own.

This list is not comprehensive, but it does work as a good starting point to get you thinking about your needs.

For each of the things below, you will either mark it with a one, two, three. One means you do that thing poorly, rarely do it, or never do it. Two means that you do that thing okay, or sometimes do it. Three is I do that thing very well, or I often do it. You can then mark any of these with a star, meaning that you would like to improve that item.

It's important to know that you may think you are eating healthy for people with an eating disorder, but you may not be. You could also think you are exercising a normal amount, but you could be exercising too much. Please keep these things in mind.

Physical Self-Care

- Rest when sick
- Go to doctor's appointments regularly (including the dentist)
- Get enough sleep
- Participate in fun activities
- Eat regularly (at least three meals a day)
- Wear clothes that help me feel good
- Exercise (around 150 minutes a week)
- Take care of personal hygiene (bathe regularly, brush teeth, comb hair)
- Eat healthy foods
- Overall physical self-care

Emotional and Psychological Self-Care

- Talk about my problems
- Find reasons to laugh
- Do something comforting
- Go on day-trips or vacations
- Recognize my achievements and strengths
- Express my feelings in a healthy way
- Learn new things that aren't related to school or work
- Get away from distractions
- Participate in hobbies
- Take time off from school, work, and other obligations
- Overall emotional and psychological self-care

Social Self-Care

- Keep in touch with friends
- Have intimate time with my partner
- Do enjoyable activities with others
- Ask others for help when needed
- Spend time alone with my partner
- Meet new people
- Have stimulating conversations
- Write or call family or friends who live far away

- Spend time with people I like
- Overall social self-care

Spiritual Self-Care

- Appreciate art that is impactful to me (books, film, movies)
- Participate in a cause that I find important
- Set aside time for reflection and thought
- Act in accordance with my values and morals
- Recognize the things that give my life meaning
- Pray
- Mediate
- Spend time in nature
- Overall spiritual self-care

Professional Self-Care

- Advocate for fair benefits, pay, and other needs
- Keep a comfortable workspace that lets me be successful
- Maintain work-life balance
- Take breaks
- Make time to talk and build a relationship with coworkers
- Learn new things that related to my work
- Take on projects I find rewarding and interesting
- Say no to excessive responsibilities

- Improve my professional skill
- Overall professional skills

Chapter 9:
SUBSTANCE ABUSE

An addiction is a disease characterized by using a substance despite serious substance-related problems, like losing control over use, negative social consequences, or health problems. The most common signs of addiction include:

- Loss of control over substance use
    o Experiencing cravings
    o Significant time spent using, obtaining, or recovering from the substance
    o Difficulty reducing substance use
    o Using more of the substance than you intend to
- Occupational or social problems
    o Decreasing or giving up an important job or social activities

- o Social problems due to continued use
- o Not fulfilling major home, work, or school obligations
- Risky use
  - o Psychological or physical problems caused by the continued use
  - o Using the substance in situations where it creates physical danger
- Physical effects
  - o Experiencing withdrawal symptoms when you don't use the substance
  - o Building up a tolerance and needing more to obtain the desired effect

Through the use of CBT, you can spot the automatic thoughts that cause you to feel as though you have to use a certain substance. Oftentimes, addictions are built because a person tries to self-medicate using alcohol or drugs.

Despite some preconceived notions that people have about addition, here are the facts you need to know:

1. Addiction is indeed a disease. Addiction creates changes in the functioning and structure of the brain. It is not due to poor willpower or some sort of character flaw.

2. Addiction happens slowly, and it is not always easy to notice. Many people with addiction can function well in some areas of their lives but have problems in other areas.
3. Relapse means that you return to the regular use of a substance after a certain period of sobriety. On the other hand, a lapse is a single incident of use without falling back into your old patterns.
4. Relapses can occur at any point during recovery, which is a lifelong battle. Those in recovery are at heightened risk when experiencing stressful periods.

Substance Use Assessment

When it comes to addiction, it's helpful to have an idea of which substances you could be addicted to and how long it has affected you. Below, you will find a list of substances. For the ones you have used, fill out the information underneath. Do this even if you never became addicted to the substance. If you don't know the specifics, give your best estimate.

- Alcohol
    - Age of first use:
    - When you last used:
    - Frequency of most recent use:
    - Was this substance ever a problem?

- Benzodiazepines (Xanax, Valium, etc)
    - Age of first use:
    - When you last used:
    - Frequency of most recent use:
    - Was this substance ever a problem?
- Cocaine
    - Age of first use:
    - When you last used:
    - Frequency of most recent use:
    - Was this substance ever a problem?
- Crack
    - Age of first use:
    - When you last used:
    - Frequency of most recent use:
    - Was this substance ever a problem?
- Hallucinogens (LSD, mescaline, etc.)
    - Age of first use:
    - When you last used:
    - Frequency of most recent use:
    - Was this substance ever a problem?

- Heroin
    - Age of first use:
    - When you last used:
    - Frequency of most recent use:
    - Was this substance ever a problem?
- Inhalants
    - Age of first use:
    - When you last used:
    - Frequency of most recent use:
    - Was this substance ever a problem?
- Marijuana
    - Age of first use:
    - When you last used:
    - Frequency of most recent use:
    - Was this substance ever a problem?
- Methamphetamine
    - Age of first use:
    - When you last used:
    - Frequency of most recent use:
    - Was this substance ever a problem?

- Methadone
    - o   Age of first use:
    - o   When you last used:
    - o   Frequency of most recent use:
    - o   Was this substance ever a problem?
- MDMA
    - o   Age of first use:
    - o   When you last used:
    - o   Frequency of most recent use:
    - o   Was this substance ever a problem?
- PCP
    - o   Age of first use:
    - o   When you last used:
    - o   Frequency of most recent use:
    - o   Was this substance ever a problem?
- Prescription Medicine (Vicodin, oxy, etc.)
    - o   Age of first use:
    - o   When you last used:
    - o   Frequency of most recent use:
    - o   Was this substance ever a problem?

- Other (list them out)

Next, answer each of these questions with either a yes or a no. Don't overthink your responses. If you don't know, go with your first instinct.

Have your relationships with family or friends been damaged or strained by your alcohol or drug use?

Have you had problems reducing or ending your substance use?

Have you ever missed work or had reduced productivity due to your substance abuse?

Have you ever used a substance to self-medication for anger, anxiety, depression, or other negative emotions?

Have you ever experienced strong cravings for a substance?

Have you built up a tolerance for a substance that required you to use more to reach your desired level of intoxication?

Have you operated a vehicle or engaged in a dangerous activity while under the influence?

Have you ever give up healthy or enjoyable activities due to your substance use?

Have you ever engaged in risky sexual actions while under the influence?

Have you ever experienced withdrawal symptoms, like irritability, physical discomfort, or headache due to abstinence from the substance?

Relapse Prevention Plan

When it comes to getting sober, relapse is one of the scariest things that can happen. Coming up with a relapse prevention plan can help relieve this worry.

The first thing you need to do is come up with some coping skills. List out skills or activities that you like to do to help take your mind off of using.

_____

_____

_____

Next, come up with three people you know you can talk to if you start to think about using. It is a good idea and is taught in 12-step meetings that you have a sponsor, and they should be one of these three people. They have been where you are, so they can help you more than somebody who has never experienced addiction.

_____

_____

_____

It also helps to write out consequences. How is your life going to change if you relapse? What is your life going to be like if you stay sober? Make two columns and answer those questions.

_____

_____

_____

Tips for avoiding relapse:

1. Cravings will pass. Do your best to distract yourself and ride it out.

2. Don't allow yourself to become complacent. Relapse can end up happening years after you have quit using. There will never be a time when it's safe to "just have one."
3. Avoid situations that you know could put you at risk of relapsing, like spending time with friends who still use or going places that can trigger your past.
4. The decision to relapse is only made once you place yourself in a risky situation, long before deciding to use it again.
5. Don't look at relapse as a failure. Falling back into your old patterns due to a slip is only going to make the situation worse.

Chapter 10: PHOBIAS

Phobias are unrealistic fears about something. It might be an insect, animal, situation, or object. Phobias get diagnosed when anxiety to the feared stimulus gets so intense that it causes too much stress or keeps a person functioning normally. Phobias can be treated and have the best chance of having good outcomes than other psychological issues.

There isn't a question that the best treatment for phobia is CBT. Many studies have shown that people who have a short course of CBT have the best chance of improving. Around 80 to 90 percent of people who undergo CBT for phobias show a complete remission by their tenth session. If you compare this to other talk therapies, they only have a 60 percent chance of improvement.

CBT for phobias involves un-paring the response from the fear.

CBT can do this by first finding the irrational or problematic thinking patterns. It helps you take on new ways of thinking about a challenging item or situation. When these thought patterns are more realistic and helpful, CBT can help people extinguish their response by giving them ways to help them face the fear without feeling anxious. Through CBT, most people will show improvements by the fifth session.

CBT will be different for every person and will be tailored for every person's own n-unique needs. But CBT for phobias typically involves a combination of mindfulness training, systematic exposure, and cognitive restructuring.

Examining the Evidence

Anytime the evidence that underlies a core belief gets challenged, the core belief can be changed. But this can be hard since not all evidence gets treated the same. Information that can support a core belief can be integrated easily, and this just makes the belief stronger. Information that doesn't support the belief will just be ignored.

This exercise will help you look at the evidence for and against your core beliefs, and this includes evidence that you might have rejected earlier. The exercise will teach you how to do the information processing model first by giving you examples, but there will be space where you can look at and challenge your core beliefs.

You need to have a basic understanding of core beliefs, and you need to know at least one core belief before you use this worksheet. Your core beliefs are your most central ideas about the world, others, and yourself. These beliefs will act like a lens through which each situation and life experience gets seen.

As you have new experiences, your core beliefs might change, but some experiences have a larger impact than others. Information that supports a core belief can be easily integrated, and this just makes the belief stronger. Any information that doesn't support a belief will be ignored.

What is Your Core Belief
For this part of the exercise, you have to figure out a phobia that you have.

"I hate snakes."

Now you need to make three columns on a piece of paper. In the far left column, you need to write down all the information that supports your phobia. In the middle column, you will write any information that you might have rejected before. In the far right column, you will write down any information you can change before integrating it into your core belief.

Information That Supports Your Core Belief

"Snakes can kill."

"Snakes are poisonous."

"Snakes are slimy."

Information That You Have Rejected

"Not all snakes are poisonous."

"Snakes are scaly, not slimy."

"Snakes only kill their prey."

Information That You Modified

"Not all snakes are poisonous, but all snakes have fangs and can bite me."

"Snakes can become frightened and bite me out of fear."

"Snakes are slimy when they shed their skin, so that fact is true."

Exposure Hierarchy

This is a basic CBT tool to help treat anxiety. You can use it to introduce your phobia slowly. Start by making a list of everything that you are afraid of and then estimating how severe your anxiety gets when you see that stimuli. You will slowly expose yourself to these stimuli but start with the one that produces the least anxiety.

The first thing you need to do is describe, using broad terms, all the things that make you anxious:

_____

_____

_____

Now, describe some situations that are related to your anxiety that make you feel various levels of discomfort. Using a rating of zero to ten with zero being not at all anxious and ten being extremely anxious, and rate how much these situations affect you:

_____

_____

_____

Chapter 11: TRAUMA

Many adults will have some painful memories of their past. Some of these won't be too bad, such as when you've embarrassed yourself, or you might cringe anytime you think of them years later. Then, you have the heavy stuff such as regret, loss, and heartbreak. These memories are more than just some images and facts. They carry powerful emotions that make you feel like you have been hit right in your stomach anytime they come up.

When talking about trauma, things are also taken to extremes. Traumatic memories are so filled with emotions that even some of the smallest reminders. Just hearing a car horn could send someone into a panic attack. A smell might send another person into a rage.

Most trauma survivors will try to avoid any of those memories because nobody wants to knowingly expose themselves to something that will cause them great pain. However, this act of avoiding trauma can often cause more harm than good. Trying to avoid these things could cause the trauma to be even more painful, and there are triggers that you just can't stay away from.

COIVD-19 Trauma

Trauma can also be created by things like pandemics, just like what the entire world has faced since the beginning of 2020 with COVID-19. It has upended what we have long considered "normal" life and has caused billions of people to experience an emotional turmoil that they have likely never faced before. While we might not realize it, this emotional turmoil is creating trauma in adults. This can end up causing some serious physical and mental effects if not taken care of.

It's also very common for people to downplay the traumatic nature of things like a global pandemic. After all, the word trauma is typically used to describe violent experiences. However, you don't have to experience violence to experience trauma.

One of the key indicators of PTSD is to see the world as a dangerous place. The pandemic has caused that fear in a large number of people. We feel more on guard or unsafe. For adults who have children who can't go to school because of the pandemic, added stress and worry. You also feel as though you need to protect your children from what is happening, but that's not always possible. This builds up and will affect you just like any other form of trauma.

We all have experienced a loss of routine, disruption of school, family gathers, and the inability to interact with people outside of our immediate household.

One of the most common things a therapist will do is use exposure therapy to help treat trauma. During these treatments, the patient will be confronted with reminders of the trauma slowly within an environment that is safe. By being exposed enough to the memories of the trauma, they will lose their power.

With this exercise, we will explore a single technique that is known as a trauma narrative. This is a powerful technique that lets the survivors confront their memories and overcome them through a simple story.

What is Trauma Narrative

A trauma narrative is a special type of psychological tool that can help trauma survivors make sense of the things they experienced while acting as a form of exposure therapy to painful memories.

When trauma goes untreated, it can cause a person to start feeling like a jumbled mess of images, emotions, and sounds. When performing one of these trauma narratives, your traumatic experience will be done by repeatedly telling the story through art, written, or verbal means. Expanding and sharing upon this narrative lets you organize your memories, making them more manageable, which can diminish the pain they carry.

Trauma stories can be shared by talking about it both outside and inside treatment. Sometimes this retelling might be disruptive, especially if it happens in a place that isn't appropriate, like school or work. Learning how to use trauma narratives will let you control potential problems.

Using A Trauma Narrative

Psychoeducation

Just like with any other type of exposure therapy, it is helpful to use psychoeducation first. The therapist you choose must know the basics of trauma, how important it is to treat trauma, and ways exposure therapy can work.

An overview of trauma psychoeducation goes farther than this chapter can cover, but here are some key points:

- It is perfectly normal to feel uncomfortable when you talk about your trauma. When working with a therapist, you won't ever be in any danger. If it gets too uncomfortable, you can always stop.

- After being exposed to the traumatic memories enough, they won't be as powerful.

- Trying to avoid the traumatic memories could feel right at the moment, but it will make your symptoms worse when they do pop up.

- Trauma is a very typical reaction to some experiences, and how each person will handle this is going to be unique.

Creating a Narrative

Many trauma narratives will take several sessions to get through. How fast you are able to do this is determined by your level of comfort, how many details you can share, and your therapist's judgment.

- Begin With Facts

When you first retell your story, you need to make sure that you remain focused on exactly what happened. Go over the specifics about the traumatic experience. Trauma narratives will be more effective if you can write them down. But for some people, it is hard to get started with a blank canvas. If this is the case, talking about the specifics of the event makes it easier to help write things down later on.

If you find that the facts are too difficult to face as a whole, you can break them down. You can write down separate entries about the things that happened after, during, and before the trauma.

- Adding Feelings and Thoughts

After you have written downs all the facts about the trauma, now it is time to revise it and add in more details. Slowly read through the narrative and add in any feelings or thoughts you experienced during the trauma. You can also revise the facts during this time if you need to.

Try to stay away from any irrational or challenging thoughts right now. Use open questions that can help you explore your feelings and thoughts. Don't try to dig too deep right now. That will come later.

- Dig A Bit Deeper

As you get more comfortable telling your story, you can start focusing on the more uncomfortable parts. Try to share your worst moments or memory about the trauma. Dig as deep as you can by adding as many details as possible.

If this part is too hard right now, you can move slower. Spend some time looking over what you have written down and add more details if you can. You can use prompts like adding in things you noticed with your senses and how you felt and thought during the hardest times.

- Wrap It Up

Once you have everything written down and you have re-read it in detail, it should be a bit easier for you to talk about. You can now add in some cognitive skills. Look over your story one more time but this time, try to challenge any irrational thoughts. You can change any sections if you want to.

Now you need to write one more paragraph about how you are feeling right now as compared to when the trauma was happening. Did you learn anything? Do you feel stronger? What could you say to somebody who has gone through the same things?

Multiple Traumas

You might have experienced more than one traumatic experience, like being in an abusive relationship for a long time or served in the military during wartimes. Take some time to figure out what is included in your narrative and the things you left out.

Rather than having just one narrative, you could decide to come up with your own "life narrative," or something that has a timeline that aligns closer to the incidents. You can also create a timeline to use as a guideline and then focus on a single experience.

Common Reactions To Trauma

Reactions to trauma can be painful, personal, and unique. There might be times when a reaction seems random like it doesn't have anything to do with the trauma. At other times, they are just too much. These can be overwhelming, painful, and vivid. The first step in most trauma interventions involves making these reactions normal while showing them that they aren't alone, wrong, or broken.

This exercise lets you summarize common reactions and symptoms that most people experience after trauma. The main goal of this exercise is to normalize and validate your reactions to the trauma. This could have several benefits. Symptoms that might seem uncontrollable and random have now been attached to a trauma, which can build hope that they might be treated.

This exercise is best when used as a prompt for discussing your response to the trauma. Try your best to describe your behaviors, feelings, and thoughts that you have experienced since the trauma happened. You can use this resource as a roadmap to your recovery.

Re-experiencing the Trauma

You could re-experience your trauma through memories, feelings, thoughts, or other ways. Re-experiencing your trauma could be extremely distressing and could trigger emotions that might be uncomfortable, like sadness, anger, or fear.

You might experience:

- Physical responses or emotional distress after experiencing a reminder about the trauma
- Distressing feelings and thoughts about the trauma
- Flashbacks
- Nightmares

Avoiding Traumatic Reminders

Since being reminded of trauma could be distressing, it is widespread for survivors to avoid these reactions. You might:

- Stay away from talking about the trauma
- Suppress any thoughts that relate to the trauma
- Avoiding things, places, and people who remind you of the trauma
- Avoiding activities that relate to the trauma

- Using alcohol or drugs to suppress any uncomfortable emotions or thoughts

Negative Feelings or Thoughts

Negative feelings or thoughts might start or get worse after you have experienced trauma. Some of those feelings and thoughts may not seem like they relate to the trauma at all. You might:

- Have excessive negative thoughts about yourself or the world
- Have temporary amnesia that relates to the trauma
- Have a hard time experiencing positive feelings
- Feel isolated or disconnected from your surroundings
- Lose interest in activities you normally like to do
- Blame yourself or others that are related to the trauma

Hyperarousal

This is how you react, or you might be feeling "on edge." This might worsen after you experience trauma. This can include a large range of psychological and physical symptoms like:

- Impulsive or risky behaviors
- Feeling anxious or other symptoms like headaches, upset stomach, or racing heart
- Problems sleeping
- Looking around you to see anything that reminds you of the trauma

- Problems concentrating
- Being startled easily
- Getting aggressive, angry, or irritable

Chapter 12: SELF-HARM

Research has found that CBT after a person has harmed themselves was a very effective treatment. Self-harm is an "intentional act of non-fatal self-injury or self-poisoning." This is very common, especially with adults between the ages of 15 and 35 years. This is normally repeated and has been associated with suicide. This is why people who harm themselves need to find a good therapist to help them.

Even though some people might ask for help, self-harm might be discovered by friends or family. Your doctor might find evidence of self-harm when doing a routine exam, like fresh injuries or scars.

There isn't a definitive test to diagnose self-harm. Diagnosis is based on the psychological or physical evaluation. You might be referred to a therapist who is experienced in treating people who do self-harm.

A therapist might evaluate you for other mental health disorders that might be linked to self-harm, like personality disorders or depression. If this is the case, the evaluation might include other tools like psychological tests or questionnaires.

There isn't one way to treat self-harm, but the first step is to tell somebody you trust so you can find help. Treatment will be based on your specific problems and any other related disorders you might have. Since self-harm could become a huge part of your life, it is best to get your treatment from a mental health professional who is experienced in treating self-harm.

If your self-harm is associated with mental health disorders like borderline personality disorder or depression, your treatment plan will focus on that disorder along with your self-harm.

Treating self-harm can take some time, a lot of work on your part, and your desire to get better.

You do have some treatment options, and psychotherapy is one of them. Psychotherapy could help:

- Find healthy skills to help you solve your problems
- Create skills to help you improve your social and relationship skills
- Find ways to boost your self-image
- Find a way to handle your emotions

- Find skills to help you manage your stress
- Find and manage any underlying problems that might be triggering your self-harm

There are many types of psychotherapy that might help you like:

- Mindfulness-based therapy will help you live in each moment. It can help you perceive the actions and thoughts of the people around you to lessen your depression and anxiety while improving your well being.
- Dialectical behavior therapy: this is a kind of CBT that will teach you skills to help you handle your stress, manage your emotions while improving your relationships with other people.
- CBT can help you find all the negative and unhealthy behaviors and beliefs while replacing them with adaptive, healthy ones.

In addition to individual therapy, group or family therapy might be needed.

Suicide Assessment

You can use the suicide assessment exercise to look at different factors related to a person's risk of suicide. Each point represents a risk factor that will have a strong correlation to suicide. This exercise could help make sure you are covering important bases when questioning your suicidal thoughts while creating good documentation.

This exercise is intended to help give you a judgment about suicidal thoughts. This is in no way a diagnostic tool. You might be at risk of suicide even if you aren't exhibiting any of the warning signs.

For the list below, you will need to answer "yes" or "no" for each one:

- Family history of suicide
- Previously tried to commit suicide
- Have access to drugs, firearms, or other means of suicide
- Has a plan in place for ways to commit suicide
- Recent ideas about suicide
- Recent threats of committing suicide
- Current substance abuse
    o   If so, has the substance abuse increased
- Recent stressors like illness, loss of a relationship, financial problems

For the issues listed below, you will need to give each one a rating between one and five, with one being the least to five being extremely.

Depression

Hopelessness

Social Support

Impulse Control

Anxiety or Agitation

Safety Plan

If you feel that yourself or someone you love is at risk for self-harm or suicide, but they haven't reached the level of severity required for hospitalization, it is normal to make a safety plan.

A good safety plan can help you understand personal red flags that can tell you that you need to get help. In situations that aren't as dire, having some coping skills might work. If something more is needed, this exercise has places where you can write down people you can turn to if needed. This exercise also has some phone numbers to help you get in touch with professionals should you need them.

Safety plans have to be carefully used and with good judgment. Make sure you do the suicide assessment first.

Know When to Get Help

You need to list any warning signs that you know of when you start struggling with a problem. This could include behaviors, feelings, or thoughts.

_____

_____

_____

Coping Skills

You will need to write down things that you can do that will help you take your mind off your problems. Are there any obstacles that might keep you from using your coping skills?

_____

_____

_____

Social Support

If you can't handle your stressful mood by yourself, get in touch with family members or friends that you trust. Write down several people who you can call if your first choice isn't available. Make sure to write down their contact information, too.

_____

_____

_____

Professional Help

If your problems persist, or if you start having more suicidal thoughts, contact some professional help:

Suicide hotlines within the US:

- 1-800-SUICIDE
- 1-800-273-TALK
- 1-800-799-4889 for hard of hearing or deaf people

You can list any professionals you know of or your local emergency number below:

_____

_____

_____

Stress Exploration

Stress can be feelings of being exhausted, worn out, overwhelmed, or tense. A little bit of stress could be motivating, but too much could make the tiniest of tasks seem overwhelming. There is a time when several small problems accumulate stress, but at other times, it results from long-term problems or massive life changes.

This exercise can help you learn about your stressors and other factors that can protect you from stress. Stressors might include daily problems, huge life changes, and circumstances in life. Some things that can protect you against stress might include protective factors, healthy coping strategies, and daily uplifts.

Since stress contributes to other types of mental problems, this exercise will fit well with other treatment plans.

Factors that Can Contribute to Stress

List your largest stressors for the following categories and give them a rating of one to ten, with one being "a bit stressful" and ten beings "extremely stressful."

- Daily Problems

These will be common things that annoy your or just the strains of everyday life like arguments with your partner, no or very little free time, homework, no sleep, problems at work, chores, traffic, etc. Don't forget to give them a rating.

_____

_____

_____

- Life Changes

These will be negative and positive events that require you to make huge adjustments like injury, illnesses, moving, death, new job, divorce, the birth of a child, etc. Don't forget to give them a rating.

_____

_____

_____

- Life Circumstances

This will be any long-term or permanent circumstances that make your life harder, like living in an unsafe place, not liking your job, discrimination, values that conflict with your culture, chronic illnesses, financial hardships, etc. Don't forget to give them a rating.

_____

_____

_____

Factors that Can Protect You Against Stress

Describe things in your life that helps to counteract your stress.

- Daily Uplifts

These would be any positive experiences that make you feel happy, like spending time in nature, activities you enjoy, spending time with friends, eating your favorite foods, etc.

_____

_____

_____

- Healthy Coping Strategies

This would be any positive action that can help you manage or reduce your stress or other uncomfortable emotions like relaxation techniques, journaling, self-care, talking about your problems, exercising, etc.

_____

_____

_____

- Protective Factors

This would be any life circumstances or individual characteristics that can protect you from stress like education, motivation toward success, supportive family, good health, financial security, etc.

_____

_____

_____

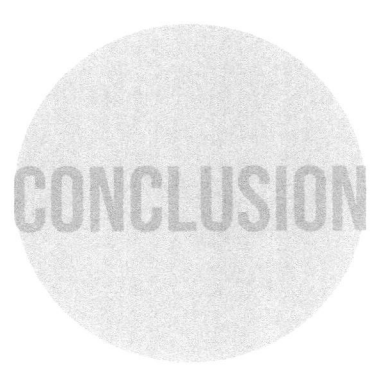

CONCLUSION

Thank you for making it through to the end of the *CBT Workbook For Adults*. Let's hope it was informative and able to provide you with all of the tools you need to achieve your goals, whatever they may be.

The next step is to start using the techniques to help improve your life and mental health. It is never too late to start bettering yourself. While it will take some time before you start seeing tremendous results, just know that your effort and time spent working on these techniques will pay off. Many of these worksheets and plans will overlap, so use whichever one you feel can help serve you the best, even if it's listed under something that you aren't troubled with. Continue to work at it, and I'm certain you will see improvement.

It can seem challenging to make significant changes to your psyche, but it is possible. All you need is an ounce of willpower to make a change in your life and in your health. If you have that ounce of willpower, you can do anything that you want to do. You can improve your life ten-fold. You can do this.

Finally, if you found this book useful in any way, a review on Amazon is always appreciated!

Printed in Great Britain
by Amazon